THE TABLETOP LEARNING SERIES

CRAYONS & MARKERS

Artistic Creations, One of a Kind and Made by You

by Imogene Forte

Incentive Publications, Inc.
Nashville, Tennessee

Illustrated by Gayle Harvey
Cover illustrated by Becky Cutler
Edited by Sally D. Sharpe

ISBN 0-86530-162-X
Library of Congress Catalog Card Number 86-82934

THE TABLETOP LEARNING SERIES™ is a trademark of Incentive Publications, Inc., Nashville, TN 37215

THIS
CRAYONS & MARKERS
BOOK BELONGS TO

_____

CONTENTS

HOLIDAYS

A NOTE TO KIDS

Kids everywhere know that crayons and markers offer unlimited possibilities for hours of creative fun and artistic exploration! Sometimes, though, because crayons and markers are so readily available, we put them aside in order to use more unusual and expensive materials.

With a little imagination, there are many exciting things you can make and do with crayons and markers. They are inexpensive, clean, easy to use and store, and can be used again and again in many different ways. You can use them almost anywhere and at any time -- inside or outside, in a car, plane or boat, in restaurants or the doctor's office, and at home or in the classroom. But perhaps the best thing about crayons and markers is that you never know how a project will turn out!

This book has been written to help you see crayons and markers in a new light. Some activities include easy, step-by-step instructions for making useful or decorative items to give as gifts or to keep for yourself. Others, however, are just for you to experiment with and enjoy. None of the activities require expensive or hard-to-find materials. If you have a new or nearly new box of crayons, a handful of old crayons, at least a dozen markers of assorted colors, scissors, a little paint, a bit of string, some paper, glue, and assorted "good junk" from around the house, you're set for loads of crayon and marker fun.

So, round up your supplies and get set to produce some old, some new, some ordinary, and some extraordinary artistic creations. The wonderful thing is that each project will be fun, one of a kind, and made by you!

Imogene Forte

SCRATCH A PICTURE

WHAT TO USE:

- peeled crayons
- newspaper
- lightweight cardboard
    or heavy drawing paper
- old ball point pen
    or knitting needle
- black tempera paint
- liquid soap
- paintbrush

WHAT TO DO:

1. Cover a work surface with newspaper.
2. Completely cover a piece of cardboard or heavy drawing paper with a heavy coating of crayon. Use many different colors. Press down firmly to make squares, circles, geometric designs, and diagonal lines.

3. Mix black tempera paint and liquid soap to make a thick "wash". Paint over the entire picture using a paintbrush. Allow the paint to dry. Use the point of a dried-up ball point pen or a knitting needle to scratch a design. Let your imagination run wild! Scratch an exotic peacock, parrot, or other bird with magnificent plumage!

WHAT IS FUN:

Prepare a "scratch a picture" using very thin paper. (Tracing paper is good.) Be careful not to tear the paper when you are scratching away the crayon. (Try using a blunt pencil instead of a pen or knitting needle.) Make a small hole at the top of the finished picture and run a string through it. Knot the end of the string and hang the picture in front of a window. As the sun shines through the window, the crayon colors will shimmer and shine!

FROM PICTURE TO PRINT

it's easier than you think!

WHAT TO USE:
- crayons
- drawing paper
- iron
- newspapers

WHAT TO DO:
1. Cover a work surface with a thick pad of newspaper.
2. Draw a design on a piece of drawing paper and color it very heavily with crayons.
3. Place a blank piece of drawing paper on the newspaper surface.
4. Lay the crayon design face down on the blank paper.

Please ask an adult for help with the iron.

5. Press the back of the design with a warm iron, moving the iron from side to side to melt the crayon onto the blank paper.
6. Carefully remove the top piece of paper. Your crayon design is now a print!

WHAT IS FUN:

You can use your original crayon design to make more than one print. Fold several prints and write holiday or birthday greetings on the insides, or make your own wrapping paper by decorating butcher paper with prints. Try mixing and matching more than one design in the same project for an especially creative flair!

SANDPAPER SAVVY

WHAT TO USE:
- crayons
- fine grain sandpaper
- drawing paper
- paintbrush
- turpentine

WHAT TO DO:
1. Draw a picture on sandpaper using crayons. Be sure to press down hard!
2. Using a paintbrush, coat a piece of paper with turpentine.
3. Place the sandpaper on the turpentine-coated paper, drawing side down.
4. Rub the sandpaper from side to side several times.
5. Remove the sandpaper to uncover a reproduction of your original drawing!

WHAT IS FUN:
You will be able to use the sandpaper drawing more than once. Decorate wrapping paper, make your own greeting cards, or design original stationery!

JUST "TOOLING" AROUND

WHAT TO USE:
- crayons
- drawing paper
- newspaper
- ball point pen

WHAT TO DO:
1. Cover a work surface with a thick stack of newspapers. (Dampen the top layer of newspapers.)
2. Place a sheet of drawing paper on the newspaper surface.
3. Using a ball point pen, draw a "line drawing" on the paper. Let the ink dry completely.
4. Fill in the line drawing with crayon. Be careful not to color over the lines! Use light and dark shades to give your design interest.

17

"WOODEN" YOU LIKE TO CRAYON ON WOOD?

WHAT TO USE:
- crayons
- piece of wood
  (cedar shingle,
  side of a fruit
  box, plywood, etc.)
- pencil
- paper
- iron

WHAT TO DO:
1. Looking at the texture
   and shape of a piece of
   wood, think of a design
   you would like to draw on
   the wood.

2. Use a pencil to draw a design on the wood.
3. Color the design with crayons, bearing down heavily. Color as much or as little of the design as you like.
4. Place a piece of paper on the wood and carefully press the paper with a warm iron. The heat from the iron will cause the crayon wax to "melt" into the wood creating a lovely muted effect.

WHAT IS FUN:

Follow the directions above to make a wall plaque for a holiday or birthday gift. Glue a picture frame hanger (from any hardware store) on the back of the wood, or make two holes in the wood and run a cord through the holes for hanging.

EXHIBIT YOUR SCHOOL SPIRIT

WHAT TO USE:
- 9 inch by 12 inch drawing paper
- crayons

WHAT TO DO:
1. Fold a 9 inch by 12 inch piece of drawing paper in half lengthwise. Open the paper and lay it on a flat work surface.
2. Use a black crayon to write the name of your school in fancy letters on one side of the paper. (Bear down hard!)
3. Fold the paper and rub hard over the paper with your fist to transfer the crayon design to the other side.
4. Open the paper. Color around the outline of the design with a bright crayon. Use other colors to continue making "outlines" around the crayon design. Add interest by making heavy lines, light lines, wavy lines, and squiggly lines.

WHAT IS FUN:
Ask every member of your class to make a school spirit design. Make a special bulletin board to "show off" the completed crayon designs. Everyone will be amazed at the different styles and colors!

RUB-A-DUB-DUB

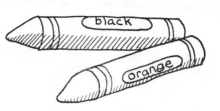

WHAT TO USE:
- crayons
- drawing paper
- objects with rough or uneven textures

WHAT TO DO:
1. Place an object under a piece of drawing paper.
2. Rub back and forth over the object with a crayon to imprint a design. Using light and heavy strokes will add shading and will provide interest to the completed print.

Note: Some objects that make interesting rubbings include automobile license plates, coins, buttons, tree bark, plastic knives, necklaces, fossils, and twigs.

21

 # COLOR ON CLOTH

WHAT TO USE:

- crayons
- piece of solid colored cloth
- newspaper
- iron

WHAT TO DO:

1. Cover a work surface with a pad of newspaper.
2. Stretch the cloth over the newspaper surface.
3. Use a yellow or white crayon to lightly sketch a design on the cloth.
4. Select crayons of the colors you would like to include in your design. Use these crayons to firmly rub your design into the cloth.

5. When you have completed your design, turn the cloth over so that the colored surface is face down on the newspaper.
6. Press the back of the cloth with a warm iron. Move the iron from side to side, using slow strokes, so that the color will "stick".
7. Carefully lift the cloth from the newspaper and turn it over to see your creation!

WHAT IS FUN:
Use your original fabric design in a most creative manner! Choose one or more of the ideas on the next two pages to make something with your fabric. Try to think of your own creative ideas!

23

SHOW IT OFF

ways to use your "color on cloth" designs

1. Frame your fabric design and hang it on the wall.

2. Make a pocket for a favorite shirt -- yours or someone else's.

3. Adorn an apron for a Mother's Day, Father's Day, or holiday gift.

5. Make a "mini" design for a hanky, scarf, or tea towel for someone special.

GRANDMA
I LOVE YOU

4. Iron the design directly onto a T-shirt or sweat shirt.

7. Make a drawstring pouch to hold only the dearest possessions.

6. Border a curtain.

25

NOTCHED, BLOTCHED AND SCRATCHED

WHAT TO DO:

1. Remove the paper from several old crayons.
2. Use a nail to carefully dig "notches" out of the crayons. Make deep scratches in some crayons and squiggly, odd-shaped gouges in others.
3. Using the sides of the crayons, make interesting line drawings.

WHAT TO USE:

- old crayons
- nail
- drawing paper

CRAYON SHAVINGS

WHAT TO USE:

- crayons
- hand-held pencil sharpener
- drawing paper
- pencil
- iron

WHAT TO DO:

1. Draw a picture on a piece of drawing paper. Use big lines to give your picture large "spaces".
2. Peel the papers off of the crayons you would like to use.
3. Twist each crayon in a hand-held pencil sharpener, letting the crayon shavings fall into a paper cup (one cup for each color).
4. Sprinkle the colors of crayon shavings within the outlines of the picture.
5. Place another piece of paper over the picture, being careful not to displace the shavings too much.
6. Carefully press the top paper with a warm iron.
7. Gently remove the top paper to unveil your crayon shaving creation.

MAKE A MASK

anyone wanting to know who you are will have to ask!

WHAT TO USE:
- crayons
- drawing paper
- masking tape
- scissors
- string

WHAT TO DO:
1. On a piece of drawing paper, draw a mask that is large enough to cover your face.
2. Give the mask two eyes, a nose and a mouth.
3. Cover all of the lines in your mask drawing with masking tape.

(Remember to cover the outline of the mask, too.) Cut pieces of tape into narrow, medium, and thick widths. Use these pieces of tape to add eyelashes, a moustache, and other interesting features!

4. Now, color over the entire surface of the drawing paper with crayons. Use different colors to make an unusual design.
5. Remove all of the tape.
6. Cut out the mask following the outside lines. Cut out openings for your mouth, nose and eyes.
7. Punch a hole on each side of the mask. Run a string through each hole and knot the end of each string. Put the mask on and tie the strings behind your head to hold the mask in place.

WHAT IS FUN:
Have a costume party and provide the supplies for your guests to make their own masks! Award prizes for the scariest and the most creative masks!

 # STENCIL IN STYLE

WHAT TO USE:
- crayons
- cardboard
- scissors
- tissues
- drawing paper

OUTLINE

CUTOUT

WHAT TO DO:
1. Draw or trace a flower, an animal, or some other interesting shape on cardboard.
2. Cut around the shape to make a square or circle.
3. Carefully cut the shape out of the center of the square or circle. Now you have two stencils.
4. Color the edges of both stencils with a heavy layer of crayon.
5. Place the cutout stencil on a piece of drawing paper. Using a wadded tissue "ball", rub the colored edges to transfer the crayon to the paper.
6. Place the outline stencil on the paper so that the edges overlap the color design you just made. Rub the colored edges of the stencil with the tissue ball as in step 5.
7. Repeat steps 5 and 6 as many times as you would like. Give your stencil picture an "allover" design.

30

IT'S A WASH

WHAT TO USE:

- crayons
- tempera paint
- paper
- paintbrush
- newspaper

WHAT TO DO:

1. Using a crayon, lightly draw a picture on a piece of paper.
2. Use crayons to heavily color the parts of the picture that you would like to "feature". Leave part of the paper uncolored to give the finished picture a watercolor effect.

3. Cover a work surface with a thick pad of newspaper.
4. Make a thin tempera "wash" by mixing one part paint with two parts water.
5. Place the picture on the newspaper surface. Brush the paint "wash" over the entire picture using light, even strokes. The paint will "resist" the crayon, allowing the crayon to show through!

WHAT IS FUN:

1. Draw and color a big, orange jack-o'-lantern. Use a thin black tempera "wash" to make a "spook-proof" Halloween picture.

2. Color a sunny spring scene with lots of bright colors -- yellow, pink, purple, red and green. Brush a light blue tempera "wash" over the picture to make a sky blue background.

3. Use a sheet of pastel construction paper and a crayon of the same color to design a picture. Color black cats or bats on black paper, purple butterflies on purple paper, or a big yellow moon and yellow stars on yellow paper. Brush an extra thin, white tempera "wash" over the picture to make a very exotic look!

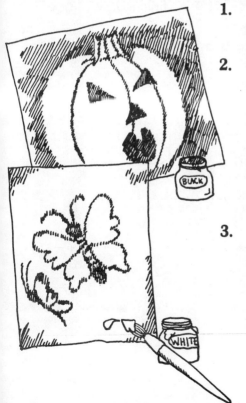

33

MARKERS

PATCHWORK PINUP

WHAT TO USE:
- markers
- wallpaper scraps
- drawing paper
- glue
- scissors
- black construction paper

WHAT TO DO:
1. Collect scraps of wallpaper with interesting designs. Look at the wallpaper carefully to find decorative patterns and unusual features.
2. Cut out a square from a piece of drawing paper. Using the square as a pattern, cut out "patchwork quilt squares" from the wallpaper.

3. Spread the wallpaper squares in front of you and begin arranging them to make an attractive design. (Try to place colors and designs that complement each other together.)
4. Use markers to draw bold, thin, wavy, straight, and "extra fancy" lines around each design or pattern on each square. Add small flowers, fancy scrolls, dots and dashes, and crazy doodles using different colors of markers.
5. As you finish a square, glue it in place on a piece of drawing paper. Continue gluing squares on the paper until all have been pasted.
6. Cut and paste a black construction paper frame around the completed patchwork design.

WHAT IS FUN:
Make a patchwork design into a book jacket for a T.V. Guide. Cut out a matching bookmark from another patchwork design to complete a special gift set for a T.V.-loving friend.

A PURR-FECT CARD

for any occasion!

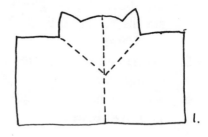

1.

WHAT TO USE:
- markers
- construction paper or drawing paper
- scissors
- glue

2.

3. YOU'RE A PURR-FECT FRIEND!

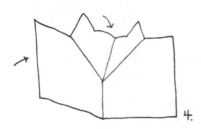

4.

WHAT TO DO:
1. Draw the card shape shown on this page on construction paper or drawing paper and cut it out.
2. Use markers to complete the cat's face. Cut a piece of construction paper into strips. Glue the strips on the cat's face to make whiskers. Remember to glue only the ends so that the whiskers will "pop out".
3. Write a greeting or message inside the card. Use one of the examples below, or make up your own message!

You're a purr-fect friend!
Thanks for the purr-fect gift!
Have a purr-fectly happy birthday!
Have a purr-fect holiday season!

38

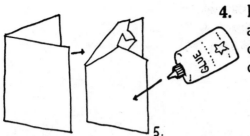

4. Fold the cat's head down along the fold lines as shown. Fold the card again to close the card. The cat's head will "pop up" when the card is opened!

5. Glue a piece of construction paper or drawing paper, the same size as the card, to the outside of the card to make a cover.

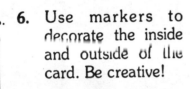

6. Use markers to decorate the inside and outside of the card. Be creative!

WHAT IS FUN:

Make other pop-up cards of your own design! You could make a valentine pop-up, an Easter egg pop-up, a menorah pop-up, or a get well bouquet pop-up. Use your imagination!

CRAZY CREATURES

with strange features

The next time you need a fun project to do with two good friends, try creating crazy creatures. All you need is a sheet of drawing paper, some markers, and lots of imagination!

First, fold a piece of drawing paper into three equal sections. Unfold the paper and prepare to make a crazy creature!

The first artist begins the crazy creature by drawing a head. When the head is complete, the first artist folds the paper and passes the drawing to the next person. The second artist adds the body, folds the paper again, and passes the drawing to the third person. The last artist completes the crazy creature by drawing legs. Unfold the paper to see your imaginative creation!

40

NAME GAMES

WHAT TO USE:
- drawing paper
- markers

WHAT TO DO:
1. Fold a sheet of drawing paper in half lengthwise. Fold the paper in half two more times.
2. Now, unfold the paper and fold it in half widthwise. Fold the paper one more time. Unfold the paper again. There should be 32 squares on the paper.
3. Write your name from left to right, one letter to a box, until all of the boxes are filled. Use a different marker color and a different design for each box!

WHAT IS FUN:
Make a "name game" design using a friend's name. Attach a birthday or holiday message for a one-of-a-kind greeting card.

WAIT, DON'T THROW THOSE OLD MAGAZINES AWAY!

Here's something fun to do with a pair of scissors, some paper, several markers, and a squirt of glue!

Flip through old magazines to find interesting faces. Cut out several faces and glue them on paper. Use markers to draw a body for each face. Add hands, arms, legs, feet, hair, clothes, and other special features. You might like to try making a collage of children's faces, people on the bus, a family picnic, etc.

MAGAZINE COLLAGE

with a different twist

Look through old magazines to find colorful and interesting pictures. Cut out the pictures and arrange them on a large sheet of drawing paper. Overlap some of the pictures, place some side by side, and leave spaces between others. Glue the pictures to the paper and use markers to add frames, decorative lines, and other drawings.

To make your collage 3-D, glue on buttons, braid, jewelry, pasta, fabric scraps, and other creative objects!

43

BOOKPLATES

leave your mark in a favorite book

WHAT TO USE:
- Contact paper or adhesive shelf paper
- markers
- scissors

WHAT TO DO:
1. Use a marker to draw a square on the right side of Contact or shelf paper. Write "This Book Belongs To _____ " inside the square. Fill the blank with your name. Decorate the bookplate with markers.
2. Cut out the square and peel away the Contact or shelf paper. Personalize one of your favorite books by sticking your original bookplate on the inside of the book's cover.

WHAT IS FUN:
Draw several bookplates on Contact or shelf paper. Write the name of a friend who loves books on the blank line and roll the paper into a scroll. Tie a ribbon around the scroll and give this special gift to your book-loving friend!

Make a bookmark to match your bookplate by sticking a rectangular piece of Contact paper to a like size piece of cardboard. Decorate your bookmark with a border or design like that on your bookplate.

MUSIC, MAESTRO

if you please

WHAT TO USE:
- record player or tape recorder
- drawing paper
- markers
- record or tape

WHAT TO DO:
1. Select a tape or record with an interesting tempo and a pleasing tune. A good selection is Haydn's "Surprise Symphony".
2. Turn the music on and listen quietly for a few minutes to "get in the mood". Begin to draw on drawing paper using markers. Draw anything the music makes you "feel"-- squiggles, squirms, curves, loops, straight lines or ragged lines. Change markers from time to time or just use one color and fill in the "spaces" with other colors. Relax, enjoy the music, and draw what you feel.

WHAT IS FUN:
Do this same activity in a group. Compare pictures to see how people react differently to the same music.

A BOX FROM NEAR AND FAR

to hold your letters!

WHAT TO USE:

- markers
- shoe box
- stamps from old letters
- construction paper or
  drawing paper
- scissors
- newspaper

WHAT TO DO:

1. Cover a work surface with newspaper.
2. Take the top off of the box. Cover the box and the top with construction paper or drawing paper. (Glue the paper in place.)
3. Collect as many different stamps from old letters as you can. Make an interesting design by gluing stamps all over the box. Be sure to spread a very thin layer of glue over

the back of each stamp to keep the glue from spreading and the stamps from falling off the box.

4. Use markers to draw outlines and borders around each stamp. Decorate the box by drawing designs and patterns.

5. Write the possessive of your name and the word "letters" on the box top. Color the letters and draw designs with different colors of markers. Now you have your very own box to hold all of your letters!

WHAT IS FUN:

Make another letter box for a friend or relative who lives far away. Write a letter to this person and put it inside the box. You can keep sending letters to completely fill the box!

HOLD ONTO YOUR ROOTS

record your family's memories

WHAT TO USE:
- markers
- drawing paper
- string or yarn

WHAT TO DO:

1. Ask an older relative, such as a parent, grandparent, aunt or uncle, to talk with you about his or her childhood. Ask questions to find out what your relative's life was like at your age. For example:

   What was your favorite hobby?
   What was your house like?
   Did you have a secret place you liked to play?
   What did your best friend look like?

   You can think of some other questions to ask. Write notes on paper to help you remember the answers.

2. Thank your relative for sharing these special memories with you.

48

3. Use markers to draw and color a picture for every answer or story that your relative told you. Try to "recapture" your relative's past in your pictures. Include as much detail as you can.

4. Punch two holes in the left side of each drawing. Run a piece of string or yarn through the holes and tie a bow to hold the pages together. Now you will always have a record of your special relative's "roots". You might like to save the drawings and share them with your relative on his or her birthday!

WHAT IS FUN:
Draw pictures to illustrate your own life and compare them to those you drew for your relative. What things are different or the same?

Interview other relatives and draw pictures to make a family "roots" book. Make a cover for your book and label the pages with names and captions.

WHEN I GROW UP . . .

a special way to appreciate your country's leaders

Do you ever daydream about what you would like to be one day? Have you ever thought that you would like to be the leader of your country?

Many countries set aside a special day each year to honor and remember the great contributions of their early leaders. Celebrate your country's special holiday by thinking about what you would like to do for your country.

Find a quiet, comfortable place where you can be alone to think. Imagine that you are the leader of your country. Use markers to draw and color a picture of yourself in this important position doing something for your country. Now imagine yourself in another role -- a

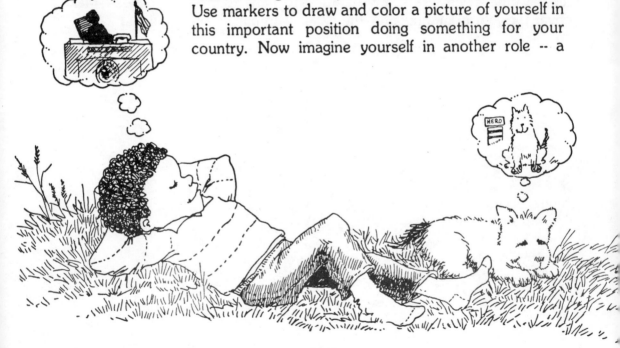

50

a carpenter, an actor or actress, an athlete, a doctor, a teacher, a pilot, or whatever you think you might like to be. Draw and color pictures of yourself in each of these roles.

Share your pictures with your family. Then, fold the pictures and put them in a large envelope. Label the envelope "When I grow up ...", and write your name and the date on the outside. Ask an adult to help you put the envelope in a place for safekeeping.

Every year or so, take out the envelope and look at the pictures. As you get older, you may want to add new pictures as your interests change. You will have fun looking at the pictures and seeing how your career goals change or stay the same! Perhaps one day you will be the leader of your country, or something equally as great!

51

IMAGINE YOURSELF

in living color

Imagine yourself in a favorite place. Think about where you are and what is around you. Now imagine what this place looks like in winter, spring, summer, and fall. Imagine yourself at this place in each of the seasons. Think about what colors you would see around you and what type of clothes you would be wearing.

Use markers to draw this special place four times on a piece of paper. Draw yourself in each picture as you would be dressed in each of the four seasons.

Now color the pictures. Let the colors show the season of each picture.

Can you imagine yourself in a land without color? What would life be like? Isn't our colorful world wonderful!

52

HANDY HAND CREATIONS

just use your hand and lots of imagination!

WHAT TO USE:
- markers
- drawing paper

WHAT TO DO:
1. Lay your hand on a piece of drawing paper.
2. Trace around your hand using a marker.
3. Make different hand prints by placing your hand palm down, palm up, fingers spread, fingers together, fist flat, fist sideways, etc.
4. Color your hand prints alive with markers. Make animals by giving hand prints fur, feathers and tails, or make unusual creatures by coloring special features!

WHAT IS FUN:
Draw and color several hand prints on heavy paper. Cut out the hand prints and glue each one to a popsicle stick. Use your hand creations to stage a puppet show!

"JUST FOR FUN" THINGS TO DO WITH MARKERS

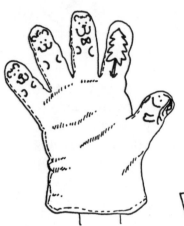

1. Turn the fingers of an old glove into puppets! Use different colors of markers to color hair, facial features, and other "distinguishing" characteristics on the fingers. Have the puppets act out a favorite fairy tale or a tall tale of your own.

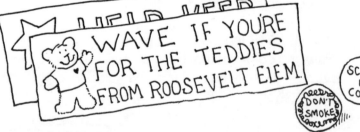

2. Design and decorate bumper stickers, buttons or posters to promote a "cause" in which you believe.

3. Make a "mask-on-a-stick". Draw a dramatic, comical or crazy face on a paper plate. Cut out eyes, a mouth and a nose. Glue a ruler or stick to the back of the plate to make a handle for the mask.

4. Make your own game board by covering an old game board or a large piece of cardboard with Contact or construction paper. Make up a game, design the game board, and write the playing rules.

5. Make a "flip" book for a younger child. Draw a picture on the lower half of the last page in the pad. Work backwards through the pad, drawing the same picture in progressing stages on the bottom half of each page. Draw the final "stage" of the picture on the first page in the pad. Flip the pages to see the action!

6. Decorate balloons for a special occasion or party. Fun party themes include circus animals, Mother Goose characters, space creatures, or cartoon characters.

HOLIDAYS

MARK UP A CARP

to celebrate the Chinese New Year

The people in China celebrate the new year with special food, lights, kites, parades, feasts, signs, and symbols. The fish, a symbol of prosperity and "the good life", is a symbol which is common during this time of festivity. One fish which is featured during the Chinese New Year is the carp.

Design your own carp to join in the celebration!

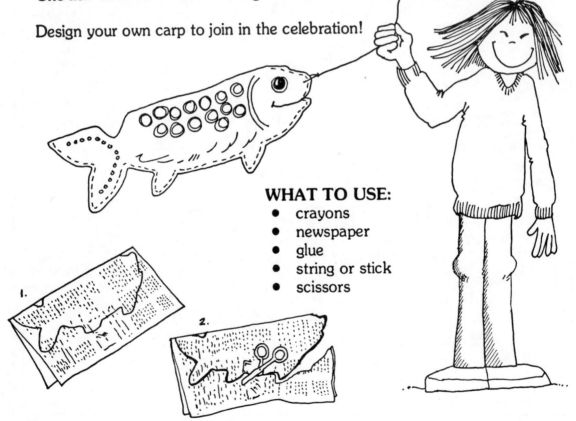

WHAT TO USE:
- crayons
- newspaper
- glue
- string or stick
- scissors

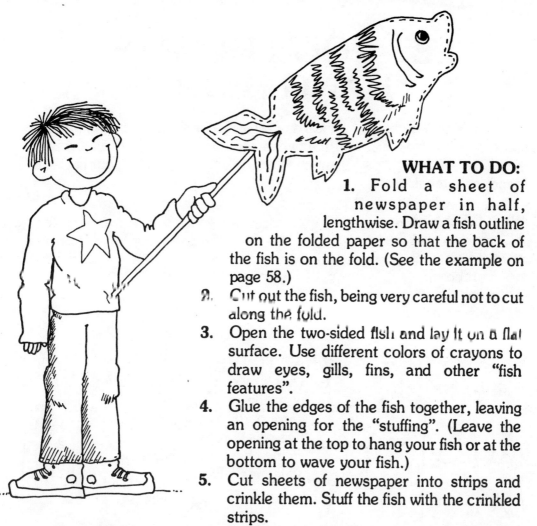

WHAT TO DO:

1. Fold a sheet of newspaper in half, lengthwise. Draw a fish outline on the folded paper so that the back of the fish is on the fold. (See the example on page 58.)

2. Cut out the fish, being very careful not to cut along the fold.

3. Open the two-sided fish and lay it on a flat surface. Use different colors of crayons to draw eyes, gills, fins, and other "fish features".

4. Glue the edges of the fish together, leaving an opening for the "stuffing". (Leave the opening at the top to hang your fish or at the bottom to wave your fish.)

5. Cut sheets of newspaper into strips and crinkle them. Stuff the fish with the crinkled strips.

6. Push a string or a stick through the opening and then staple the opening securely. Now you can join in the celebration by waving or hanging your fish!

59

♡ LET YOUR HEARTS ♡ HANG HIGH

Valentine's Day, February 14, is a day set aside for showing the people you care about how special and important they are. It's a day to celebrate friendship and love. This Valentine's Day, make a mobile for your home, a friend, or a relative!

WHAT TO USE:

- crayons
- large piece of cardboard
- string
- construction paper or drawing paper
- glue
- scissors
- scraps of fabric, rickrac, lace, doilies, sequins, etc. (optional)

WHAT TO DO:

1. Use crayons to decorate one side of a large piece of cardboard. Draw pictures, designs, patterns, etc. Remember, the theme is Valentine's Day!

2. Make one hole in the center of the cardboard and several other holes all around the card-board.

3. Run a long string through the center hole and knot the string on the decorated side of the cardboard.

4. Run a string through each hole and knot each string on the blank side of the cardboard.

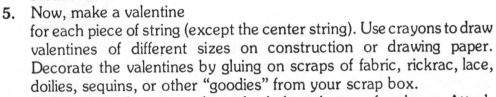

5. Now, make a valentine for each piece of string (except the center string). Use crayons to draw valentines of different sizes on construction or drawing paper. Decorate the valentines by gluing on scraps of fabric, rickrac, lace, doilies, sequins, or other "goodies" from your scrap box.

6. Cut out the valentines and punch a hole at the top of each one. Attach the valentines to the mobile by tieing a string through each valentine. Hang your valentine mobile by taping the center string to the ceiling.

WHAT IS FUN:

Write valentine messages on each valentine and give the mobile to a friend, brother or sister, or favorite adult. Or, make a valentine mobile as a class project. Each classmate can make a valentine for the mobile!

A LEPRECHAUN DRESSED IN GREEN

light green, dark green, green in-between --
the greenest leprechaun you've ever seen!

WHAT TO USE:
- crayons
- construction paper - 3 shades of green
- white construction paper
- glue

WHAT TO DO:
1. Draw the *outline* of a leprechaun on a piece of white construction paper. Use your imagination to draw the leprechaun, or look at the picture on this page to get an idea of how a leprechaun might look.
2. Now, draw the leprechaun's pants, jacket and shirt. Draw a hat on the leprechaun's head.

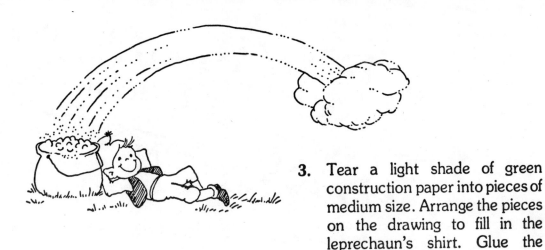

3. Tear a light shade of green construction paper into pieces of medium size. Arrange the pieces on the drawing to fill in the leprechaun's shirt. Glue the pieces in place.

4. Tear a darker shade of green construction paper into large pieces. Arrange the pieces on the drawing to fill in the leprechaun's jacket and pants. Glue the pieces in place.

5. Tear the darkest shade of green into small pieces. Arrange the pieces on the drawing to fill in the leprecaun's hat. Glue the pieces in place.

6. Use different colors of crayons to draw in the leprechaun's face, hair, ears, hands, and shoes. You might even want to draw buttons on the leprechaun's shirt and a pipe in his mouth or hand.

WHAT IS FUN:
Use crayons to draw a scene behind the leprechaun. You could color a rainbow and a pot of gold, or you could draw the leprechaun's "home" as you imagine it to be!

EASTER EGGS ON PARADE

fancy eggs to show off and hide!

WHAT TO USE:
- eggs
- egg cartons
- markers
- scissors
- glue and/or tape
- cardboard
- construction paper
- pipe cleaner (optional)

WHAT TO DO:
1. Boil the eggs in a pan of water until they are hard inside (about 10 minutes). Boil as many eggs as you would like to decorate.
2. Pour the water out of the pan and run cold water over the eggs.

3. Use many different colors of markers to decorate the eggs. Use your imagination to create out-of-the-ordinary Easter eggs. Make some eggs look like chicks by coloring a beak, small eyes and wings. Turn some into bunnies by drawing a small nose and whiskers. Give the bunny eggs large ears by gluing on ear-shaped pieces of construction paper. Draw happy, sad, and funny faces on other eggs. And, just for fun, decorate a few eggs in the traditional way -- with lines, zigzags, and dots!

WHAT IS FUN:

Show off your decorated eggs in egg carton pedestals and carts! To make a pedestal, cut one section out of an egg carton. Use markers to decorate the pedestal with colorful designs, or glue a decorated piece of construction paper around the egg carton section. To make a cart, cut the bottom of an egg carton in half. Cut four sections of cardboard to fit around the carton and tape or glue each piece of cardboard in place to make a cover for the cart. Now, decorate your Easter egg cart with pastel Easter colors! You might like to glue on cardboard wheels and bend a pipe cleaner to tape on the front for a handle.

A COLORFUL CRAYON CREATION

to celebrate Arbor Day

The United States observes one day each year for tree-planting. This special day is called Arbor Day. Many people across the United States plant trees every Arbor Day to help preserve a very beautiful and important natural resource.

Celebrate Arbor Day and the beauty of trees by creating your own colorfully "crayoned" tree. Place a piece of white drawing paper over a leaf and rub over the leaf with a crayon. Use different leaves and different colors of crayons to make several leaf prints. Cut around the leaf prints to make "leaves". Use a brown crayon to draw a big tree on a piece of white drawing paper. Now, glue the leaves onto the tree limbs. The bright colors of the leaves will make your tree a very colorful "celebration"!

SHOW YOUR SHADOW FOR GROUNDHOG DAY

There is a superstition that the groundhog's shadow predicts the weather. If you're not familiar with this superstition, find out more about it.

Celebrate Groundhog Day by "showing your shadow". Ask a friend to help you.

WHAT TO USE:
- large piece of paper (butcher paper is good)
- markers
- pencil

WHAT TO DO:
1. Sit sideways in a chair which is against the wall.
2. Have a friend tape a large piece of paper on the wall, level with your head.
3. Place a lamp behind you so that the light causes your shadow to fall on the paper.
4. Ask your friend to outline your face by tracing the lines of your shadow with a pencil.
5. Take the paper off the wall and trace the outline with a dark marker.
6. Use different colors of markers to color your hair and facial features.

WHAT IS FUN:
Turnabout is fair play. Help your friend "show a shadow", too!

I REMEMBER WHEN ...

Make an "I Remember When . . ." poster to give to a special grandparent on Grandparent's Day. Cover the poster with pictures and words that describe special things about your grandparent (hobbies, interests, habits, characteristics, life history, etc.), or special events you've shared together (trips, holidays, birthdays, stories, family gatherings, special visits, etc.).

Cut pictures and words out of magazines and paste them on the poster. Use markers to draw and write other pictures and words. Create an interesting arrangement of both magazine cuttings and marker creations. Add a final touch of color by drawing borders, geometric designs, and other "features". Try to make everything on the poster reflect the "personality" of your special grandparent!

On the back of the poster, write a special message to your special grandparent!

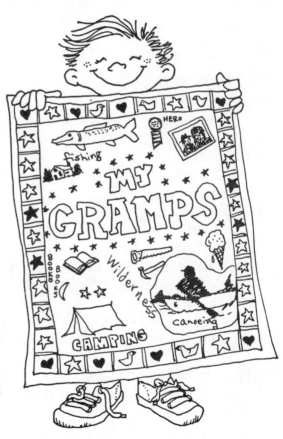

IT MUST BE HALLOWEEN

WHAT TO USE:
- black construction paper
- paintbrush
- pencil
- black crayon
- white tempera paint

WHAT TO DO:
1. Using a pencil, draw a Halloween scene with cats, witches and bats.
2. Trace over the lines of the drawing with a black crayon. (Press down hard!)
3. Mix white tempera paint with water to make a very thin "wash". Use a paintbrush to paint over the entire surface of the paper. The picture will stand out clearly to "say" that it must be Halloween.

WHAT IS FUN:
Reverse colors to make a black on white Halloween picture. Use a white crayon to draw ghosts, goblins, skeletons, and a scary cat on white paper. Paint over the paper with a black tempera "wash". Hang both Halloween pictures side by side on your front door to welcome the Halloween trick or treaters!

FANCIFUL FEATHERS

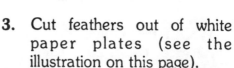

WHAT TO USE:
- markers
- brown and blue construction paper
- glue
- scissors
- pencil
- tracing paper
- white paper plates

WHAT TO DO:
1. Trace the turkey's body on the next page on a piece of tracing paper and cut out the pattern.
2. Place the pattern on a piece of brown construction paper, trace around the pattern, and cut it out.

3. Cut feathers out of white paper plates (see the illustration on this page).
4. Decorate each feather using colorful markers. Remember, this is a "fanciful" turkey!
5. Place the turkey's body on a piece of blue construction paper.
6. Arrange the feathers under the turkey's back.

7. Carefully lift the turkey's body without moving the feathers, cover the back of the body with glue, and glue it in place over the feathers.

8. Use markers to draw the turkey's eye, beak, wing, legs, and wattle (the red skin that hands under the turkey's head). Now you have a fanciful turkey to help you celebrate Thanksgiving!

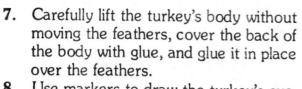

WHAT IS FUN:

To make an even more fanciful turkey, use a bright color of construction paper for the turkey's body! Use markers to draw and color a background scene around the turkey.

THE STORY OF CHANUKAH

WHAT TO USE:
- crayons and markers
- butcher paper
- ribbon or yarn
- glue

WHAT TO DO:
1. Fold a sheet of butcher paper like an accordion to make an eight-page booklet (see the pictures on these two pages).
2. Copy the "explanations" listed below, one on each page, and use crayons to draw the suggested pictures.

    page 1:   *"The Story of Chanukah".*
                (Decorate the title page however you like.)

    page 2:   *Chanukah, often called the Festival of Lights, is a special Jewish holiday which is celebrated in December. This holiday is the celebration of the cleansing of the temple many years ago. When an army surrounded the temple, the people inside had enough oil for only one day, but the oil burned for eight days!*
                Draw a temple.

page 3:   *The menorah, a special candelabra of nine candles, repre-*
          sents the eight days that the oil burned. One candle is used
          to light the other candles.
          Draw a menorah.

page 4:   *An important part of Chanukah is celebrating the holiday as*
          a family.
          Draw a family.

page 5:   *Another special way to celebrate Chanukah is by preparing*
          special foods such as latche, a potato pancake.
          Draw a latche.

page 6:   *A game often asssociated with Chanukah is the dreidel, a*
          spinning top.
          Draw a dreidel.

page 7:   *A very special part of Chanukah is reading from the Torah.*
          The Torah is the first five books of the Old Testament. A
          Torah looks like a scroll.
          Draw a Torah.

page 8:   Use crayons to decorate the last page of your booklet.

3. Glue a piece of ribbon or yarn to each end of your booklet. Fold the pages and tie the booklet together.

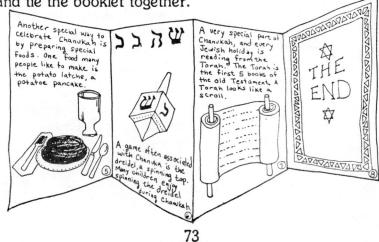

DO-UP A DOOR IN HOLIDAY FINERY

WHAT TO USE:
- markers
- butcher paper
- green and red tissue paper
- glue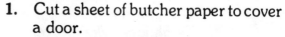

WHAT TO DO:
1. Cut a sheet of butcher paper to cover a door.
2. Using markers, draw an outline of a door on the paper.
3. Use a marker to draw the outline of a large wreath in the center of the door. Draw a bow at the bottom of the wreath.
4. Cut squares out of green and red tissue paper.
5. Squirt a drop of glue on the wreath and then cover the glue with a green tissue square. Crumple the sides of the tissue to make a "ball". Continue adding green tissue squares until the wreath is covered. (Be sure not to cover the bow.)

6. Now, cover the bow with squares of red tissue paper in the same manner.

7. Complete your holiday door by using markers to draw a border or trim around the edges of the door. Add other decorative "trimmings" with colorful markers. Complete your creation by writing your own "colorful" message to herald the holiday season.

WHAT IS FUN:

Ask your teacher if your class can "do-up a door" for your class. Each classroom might like to make a holiday door cover for a school-wide contest!

Wishing you a Super-duper wonderful, merry, jolly, holly, day!

SANTA'S HERE

Christmas must be near!

Santa needs your help! Santa's red suit doesn't fit him anymore. All of the treats that little boys and girls leave for him -- and Mrs. Claus's good cooking -- have made Santa too big for his suit. Help Santa's helpers design a new red suit for him.

Trace Santa's face using tracing paper or a thin piece of paper. Then, cut out the face to make a pattern. Trace around the pattern on a piece of drawing paper. Use markers to draw in Santa's facial features. Now, draw and color Santa's new red suit with your markers. Just for fun, glue on cotton balls to give his suit and hat a fluffy white trim!

You can make a "Santa" Christmas tree ornament by gluing your Santa drawing to a piece of heavy paper or cardboard and then trimming the Santa figure. Punch a small hole in Santa's hat and run a piece of yarn through the hole to make a loop for hanging. Santa will look great on the Christmas tree in his new red suit!

INDEX